This is the
Heart Work
of

_____

Maximize YOUR Impact

Discover Your HeartWork

Gail Carlock

Dedication

I NEVER WANTED to depend on a man.

Marry one ... yes.

Live to serve one ... no!

Through grace and grit,
we celebrate 30 years.

Now it's my honor to serve and love you!

Rogie Carlock,

thank you for walking through

this amazing life with me!

Spencer Carlock and Kullen Carlock,

you are and will always be

my greatest blessings!

May we serve and grow together!

Goliath, my fur baby in heaven,

I want to live my life like you...

full of passion, knowing to whom I belong,

and connecting with anyone who crosses my

path with love and joy!

Love, MOM.

Contents

♥ Impact Leadership

WHAT DOES IT mean to be an impactful leader? How do you equip, empower, and inspire others to live an impactful life? Living a life of impact begins with YOU. It is never what we say that moves others to action. It is what we do that others see and model. You can have the best message or product in the world, but if you don't have passion and purpose, it is hard to be available and present when others connect with you. If you haven't identified your strengths and your talents, how will you share your gifts with those you encounter each day? Without knowing your value or what you bring to others, you will be unable to live with purpose. Your passion and your purpose are the keys to knowing, understanding, and living your HeartWork!

Impact Leadership will help you identify your passion, understand your purpose, prepare you for what others bring to you, and give you a guide for living your HeartWork.

❤️ Find Your Passion

"The things you are passionate about are not random. They are your calling."

-Anonymous

SO MANY PEOPLE are searching for true passion. We want to live with passion. We want passion in our personal and professional lives. What does a passionate life look like? How do we know what our passion is, and how do we identify it? Before we can live and be passionate, we have to find out the desires of our hearts. What motivates you each day, and what ultimately gives you and brings you joy? What experiences come to mind that spark happiness? Passion is revealed in our journeys. What we have walked to and through is a part of our story.

Your path may not look like anyone else's path, and that is okay. Not all experiences evoke joy. In fact, sometimes it is easier to remember the pain and not the highlight reel. Every step we take, every situation we encounter, every person's life we help shape leads us closer to our passion. I have learned my greatest lessons on the most difficult roads I have journeyed. These detours have defined my experiences and have become a part of my story, ultimately driving me to be the best I can be every day and pushing me to pursue the desires of my heart!

Passion takes all forms in our individual lives. Passion can change from day to day or from one season in our life to the next. Even though our passion is demonstrated in different ways, there is a common theme that connects our life moments. How we identify our life moments and what we claim to be our source of joy, energy, and life is where our passion surfaces.

When asked what our passion is, we quickly share statements about what we love to do, what we have experienced, and where we have been. Passion is more than enthusiasm or excitement. Passion is fuel. Passion means that while you are completing the task, you are giving the task more energy than is required to do it. Passion is ambition that is materialized into action. What do you put more heart, mind, and soul into than anything else? That is passion defined. That kind of passion is contagious. It fuels a life of intention and propels you into moments that set you up for success. Individuals crave passion, and they follow others that possess it. They are drawn to it and want to experience all that it has to offer.

So how do you define your PASSION? As I was going through the process of defining my passion, I began to take notice of the topics I discussed with others. What did I speak most of when I engaged others? I started logging what experiences I was frequently drawn to. What daily and weekly experiences had become habits? What did I long to do but wasn't making time to do? As I scrolled through my photo albums, which situations, adventures, or people sparked joy? What was I purchasing from Amazon?

By taking notice of what I spoke most of and how I engaged others in conversation, I experienced clarity and revealed I have a heart for people. I like uncovering what motivates and drives individuals to personal and professional success. Through reflection, I began to see themes emerge. The more I was present and journaling my thoughts and topics of conversation, the more I realized my family, my boys, our adventures, and our moments together were at the heart of all my encounters. Personal enrichment and personal development growth topics, as well as nature, were my strong second. I found my passion themes did not change in the different seasons of my life. My reflection highlighted and revealed my passion is centered on PEOPLE! I am the girl that can't walk by someone without making eye contact and saying "Hi." In mid-Missouri, that task isn't as hard as it is on the streets of Manhattan. Whether I am in nature, enjoying the lake, walking on the beach, hiking, or enjoying wine with friends, I am most fueled, real, and alive when I am investing in the lives of others!

What moves me to action? Personal and professional development of myself and of others is what drives me to recognize and record the moments of my life. I truly love investing and helping others get from where they are to where they want to be. Tom Ziglar often says, "We are in the transportation business," helping others on their life journeys. Each coaching client enriches my life, helps me grow, and better equips me to help others.

We all have our own issues, obstacles, and fears. Ironically, we face many of the same hurdles. They just come in different packages. One client may want to grow his or her business and help his or her team build a culture that fosters mentoring and leadership. Another may want to focus on a specific account and strategic direction. Either way, the discussion always starts with "Why?" This then leads to passion, purpose, and connection.

Where do I invest my time, talent, and treasures? Uncovering your passion is like peeling an onion. There are many layers, and each layer brings you closer to identifying what really makes you live. Looking at where I invest my time, my talent (strengths), and my treasure (income) further refined the details of my passion. In the seasons of my life, my time was focused on different areas like my boys, their sports, their friends, and my career. Now that I am an empty-nester, I have focused more on enrichment: exercise, reading, having coffee with friends, and just being still. For so many years, I was on the treadmill of life. Each day, every moment was filled to the max. I made the most of that whirlwind, and I lived more moments than anyone running in my lane. But today I enjoy just being where my feet are planted in the moment.

Being present and soaking in people, places, and experiences fills me up, brings me joy, and slows me down. The moments are really the days of our lives. Once again, people are my time investment and a common theme for my passion. See how this process is unfolding. It is a process, a journey, to understanding and being able to verbalize your passion. Where do I invest my talents? In order to invest my talents, I have to know what they are. In my personal and professional life, I have always been a big picture, strategic person. I have been able to see the good in others and have been able to help others identify and go after their goals.

So where do I invest this super power? My investment is in the lives of my family, friends, my clients, and sometimes strangers.

I really can talk to anyone. People are so very good, if you just give them the chance to be. As far as my treasures and where I invest my income, I am a gift giver. I recognize and remember individuals not because they need it or want it, but because I enjoy doing it. As I travel, I may come upon a special token that reminds me of a certain someone. Instead of just saying, "Oh, Glenda would love that," I buy it and gift it. It is so much fun sharing these moments with the receiver. Investment in others can be as simple as a heart token or a book of matches for a friend that collects matchbooks. The point is they are thought of, and I took action to acknowledge them. The theme that keeps recurring in my life is "people."

In conversations, I speak to my adventures and experiences the most. Just this morning, I was sitting in an open-air coffee shop enjoying the sights and sounds of the French Quarter. An individual sat at the round table next to me, and a bus filled with young students passed by the balcony where we were both sitting. We waved and smiled at the students going by, and then we laughed. He asked what I was working on, and I shared my enrichment project, Impact Leadership. I asked him what his passion was. We began discussing why his passion had meaning (purpose), and then the connection that helps him live his HeartWork or calling. Why? Because I really wanted to know his story. You never know who you will meet in a coffee shop.

As you think about your passion, what moves you to action? What do you love to do? Look back at the situations and the environments that created a sense of fulfillment. When did you feel safe, alive, and free? Fulfillment allows us to be happy, and happiness gives up hope. Ultimately, passion lives in the whispers of our heart! Are you listening to the whispers?

Find your Passion!

What moves you to action?
What are your strengths?
Where do you invest your time,
talent, and treasure?
In conversations,
what do you speak to the most?
What would you do if no one paid you?

Focus on Your Purpose

"The two most important days in your life are the day you were born and the day you find out WHY!"

-MARK TWAIN

WHY AM I here? I have asked myself this question many times in my life. Seeking answers for a life moment helps define a sense of direction. Feeling lost or not a part of a bigger purpose can leave us wandering and wondering why!

"Why" helps define intention and direction. "Why" helps focus on the goal that needs to be accomplished by giving the goal meaning. For many years, I lived in a "what" world. What I did, my title, and my possessions defined me. As I developed, implemented, and accomplished my goals, I would feel rewarded and then empty. I hid behind my title and my role. I was a master mask-wearer. I would be what I needed to be in any given situation, at home or at work. Call it survival, but I was not living my authentic life. I did not know how to be vulnerable, and I could not verbalize why I was on the path I was on at that time.

In 2015, I was introduced to the Start with Why concept by Simon Sinek. I remember feeling like I had been living under a rock for too long. The concept was so simple but so very hard to implement. My "what" was strong, and my "why" scared me. The workshop forced me to dig deep, take off my masks that I had been hiding behind for years, and do the work to bring me closer to my purpose. Working to define my "why" changed my behavior. I began to look at my daily actions, goals, and life differently.

Defining my "why" gave me meaning and understanding as to why I get up every day and what I was put on this earth to do. I now have a mission all of my own, and I know why I need to live it! My "why" statement:

Transforming to connect personal and professional legacies, so that together we can reinforce, strengthen, and encourage others by heart with heart!

My "why" defined the intention by which I needed to act. Intentionality guides our life decisions and influences our behavior. Behavior shapes goals, and goals help contribute to a higher purpose. When I am working toward my "why," my strengths, talents, and gifts have meaning. When I am working to contribute to a higher purpose, I have a healthy outlook on my home, my work, and my life. Working for a greater cause gives me a sense of purpose as to why I was put on this earth. Contributing to a greater cause creates increased passion and gives your walk purpose.

How do you find your "why"? Your passion helps lead you to your purpose. What are the action words that define you? A few of the action words that resonate with me are empower, equip, reinforce, investment, strengthen, encourage, and inspire. You would think listing action words that describe you would be easy, but declaring your strengths, the words that define you, is a process. It takes reflection, focus, and vulnerability. I aspire to be one who equips, inspires, and empowers others to live lives of significance! Significance will lead to legacy, and legacy will change not only your life, but the lives of all the individuals you impact and the lives they impact. Mental blocks are real when you take the time to invest in yourself. Be patient. Look back at your passion exercise. What do you love? What sets your heart on fire? Those actions are your action words.

The next step is centered on contribution. When you live your action words, how will the people around you benefit? For example, if I help equip, inspire, and empower those I encounter personally and professionally, together we will transform lives. Transformation is my contribution. Contribution gives you a deep sense of joy. How do I contribute?

My "why," and ultimately my purpose— why I was put on this earth—is:

> To _equip_, _empower_, and _inspire_
> others so that together
> we can _transform lives_.

Now you try it.

My "why," and ultimately my purpose—why I was put on this earth—is:

> *To* ____, _____, _____
> *others so that together*
> *we can* _____*!*

Intentionality gives purpose wings. Your "why" defines your life mission statement. Your purpose is not only for you. It's for your family, your friends, your co-workers, and even strangers. Intentionally sharing your "why" shares a piece of your heart. Your HeartWork becomes actionable, and your purpose has words!

Being grateful for the beauty around me, the struggles I have survived, the pain I have passed through, and the lives I have had the opportunity to touch gives me purpose. Even failure becomes fuel that propels you to greater growth, because you believe in your "why." The act of remembering and realizing helps me look to the future with hope, trusting I will be abundantly provided for yet again. I don't know why we walk through the struggles and the pain. What I do know is that I have been carried through the hardest times in my life, and focusing on the hearts of this world has given me peace, strength, direction, and YES, blessings in the moment. What you express gratitude for today will bless you tomorrow!

My hope is that as you continue to look for the good and see the abundance in the moment, the burden of your heart's pain will be lifted. As you walk through today, know you are unstoppable. Have trust and comfort knowing you have what it takes to accomplish your purpose!

Once your purpose is defined, it is very important you embrace your purpose!

That we walk toward our "why" with intentionality and excellence.

There is only one you, with your calling, your "why," your purpose.

Believe in yourself, and then others will, too!

Focus on your purpose!

Why are you here?

What action words define you?

What is your contribution

to those you serve?

What moves you to action and brings joy?

What have you overcome

so you can inspire others?

What is the driving force in your life?

♥Identify Your Connections

"People will forget what you said, people will forget what you did, but people will never forget how you made them FEEL!"
-MAYA ANGELOU

RELATIONSHIPS ARE GIFTS. We were created for connection and meaningful exchanges of information. The moments we share are not just moments. They are the lives we have been entrusted with to live.

Each individual we meet has a unique gift that can enrich our lives, if we allow them to connect with us. Being present requires us to see the good in others. Are you a good finder? Believing the best of others and acknowledging that others are not against you is a practice. My Aunt Tannie says, "Gail, there are no accidents." Our connections are intentional moments to be valued and respected. If we choose to respond to our connections as intentional partnerships instead of interruptions, we allow our minds to shift. The disruptions of our lives become opportunities to impact the lives of others. Each of us has an emotional wake. How do others experience you? What life impact are you making?

Our gifts, experiences, and journeys identify our talents. The "whys" behind our gifts define our purpose, and those individuals who are brought into our paths are our connections. What do others bring to you? Others can identify our strengths, passions, and purpose sometimes better than we can! One of my mentors opened doors for me to serve with confidence in areas I never knew I was equipped to serve in. Professionally and personally, my coaching clients have needed to close the sales gap and acknowledge that their personal struggles, if not addressed, would affect their professional growth. My mentor knew that if he paired me with these individuals, each of us would grow. My strengths (passion) and my "why" (purpose), paired with individual (connection), has moved me toward greater growth and to a higher personal and professional performance level compared to if I had journeyed alone.

Could these coaching clients have achieved their goals without me? YES! Could they have acquired the skills necessary to win without me? YES! Were there benefits in working together on a common goal? YES! Connection allowed each individual to experience accountability and a guide to walk alongside them on their growth journey. Together, the connection maximized the impact to shorten the personal and professional gap. Connection gives each of us the opportunity to identify our strengths (passions), helps us identify and live our "whys" (purpose), and allows us to serve others through our contributions. Our gifts, our talents, our purpose, and the people we connect with are intentional tools to fuel hope. In the process of moving toward your passion, your purpose, and your connections, your calling is revealed. Then our hearts true work comes alive!

Each individual has a unique gift that can enrich the lives of others. Who do you encounter daily? Why are they in your circle of influence? Those who cross our paths are supposed to be there. There are no accidental meetings. As we encounter others on our journey, we should be open to why we cross paths with them. Many times in my life, I have been put in another person's journey to walk with them. Many times, others have been put in my path to encourage and support me.

Connection is one of life's greatest gifts. What do others bring to you? When you stop and take time to be present in the conversations you have daily, what are others talking about? I grow more one-on-one than I do in group interactions. Focused conversations allow accountability, vulnerability, and questions that uncover and reveal real needs. Our journeys give us unique experiences and skills to help others along on their journeys. Sometimes connections are made not because we have already experienced what others are going through, but because we can comfort them and have a heart of compassion.

Who is in need around you? How can you slow down and serve? A wholehearted life positively impacts the people around them. What have you been equipped and called to do with the individuals that cross your path? Connection and community begin with recognizing the needs of others. What if you are the only person who can make a difference in another's life? Ask yourself what really matters.

What impact are you having today in the lives of others? We grow through each connection we open our hearts to!

As I reflect on the connections I have made over the years, I know that I always receive more than I have ever given. Many of my coaching clients have become lifelong friends. They are friends who encourage, support, and celebrate me! Giving of yourself allows you to have faith and hope that we are enough.

Believing we are equipped to serve allows individuals to receive exactly what they need most in the moment. What others bring to you reveals the condition of your heart. So many are hurting, lost, have no hope, and are seeking direction. Impactful connections cause us to pause and ponder. What do others need? How can I be what they need me to be?

I will never claim to have all the answers, but I will do my best to be available, willing, and obedient to the needs of those who are placed in my path. We can influence and impact the lives of those around us. I recognize the responsibility now more than ever. I have this day, this moment, and if my path reveals an opportunity to connect, I am going to act in faith and make it happen.

Heart warriors invest in others with true connection. They listen, solve problems, comfort in trials, and offer unconditional love and encouragement. We are equipped to serve in whatever area God puts in our path. Trust Him! Know your strengths are made stronger in Him. What impact are you making in the lives of others?

Identify your connections!

Are you a good finder?

How do others experience you?

What impact are you making?

What do others bring to YOU?

What problems do you help solve?

What keeps you from giving time
and attention to others?

How can you slow down and Serve?

♥ Live Your HeartWork

"You can have everything you want in life if you will just help enough other people get what they want!"

-Zig Ziglar

IMPACT LEADERSHIP IS the intersection of passion, purpose, and what others bring to you in connection or in relationships with others. No one succeeds alone. We are all the sum of the experiences, influences, and people we encounter. HeartWork is fueled by passion, motivated by purpose, and strengthened by connection. Have you ever been around someone whose JOY is contagious? How does that individual make you feel? Have you ever had someone truly see you for who you really are, the good and bad, and still love you? Have you been around an individual who brings life to you and those they encounter, who helps you be a better person than you were before?

You know when you meet one of these individuals. They leave a footprint on your heart. It doesn't matter where they live, what they drive, or what clothes they wear. Their smile greets you! Their eyes have a special sparkle, and they seem to have it all together. When I am in the presence of one of these energy ambassadors, I WANT what they have! What foundation of happiness are they filling their lives with, and how can I get access to the source?

I recently crossed paths with an Uber driver who radiated joy! As I got to know her on our drive to the airport, her story intrigued me. Her accomplishments, her family, her focus, and her determination to do whatever it takes to accomplish her goals encouraged me.

Her road was not paved. In fact, her obstacles had been many. Great loss, sorrow, disappointment, and poor self-image all created setbacks, but she continued to push forward. She said, "Gail, we all have problems, but I CHOOSE JOY! I have a gift and someone needs me to share it with them today. So whatever I am facing, I will smile, rise, and be the best I can be because someone needs my sparkle!" What a gift!

These moments are what my girlfriends and I call "God Whispers," a glimpse of greatness that if recognized and implemented can change our life course forever. We crossed paths for a reason that day. Our connection was not an accident. Her heart wisdom has become the cry of my heart! Choose joy, Gail! Don't let anyone steal your sparkle, and continue to live your HEART WORK because someone needs it!

HeartWork will bring wins in business and life. President's Club trophies will be won, but after the award fades, HeartWork is lasting. HeartWork invests in the lives of those you encounter. Tom Ziglar shared this quote at our May *Choose to Win* conference:

> "Your Calling is not meant to fit
> who you are today,
> but who God created you to become!"

When I heard this quote for the first time, I had an "ah ha" moment. I always felt mismatched in my career. Why was a communications/religion major running a medical device business? Why did I have to give so much time and family sacrifice to succeed? My strength was not in the clinical realm. My strength was in hiring amazing people to clinically serve our patients and doctors, which allowed me to strategically run a very successful team.

Your calling, your HeartWork is the investment. Are you going to live it?

HeartWork is worth the effort. The investment in the lives of others, lives on to impact those around the invested. HeartWork takes time, dedication, and intentional effort.

In whom are you investing today?

We have each been given gifts ... what we are good at, what comes easy to us. Our talents are God's gifts to us, and what we do with them are our gifts to the world. When we feel complete and able to offer others guidance and hope, those strengths give us joy and happiness and allow us to serve and give others a part of who we are, and in turn, give us purpose. In my executive coaching and speaking career, I encounter men and women who are successful in their communities and companies. They are on top of their game, yet they too have a hard time recognizing and recording their strengths and gifts.

We all have a tendency to identify what we need to work on, our weaknesses, but we fail to emphasize what we do better than anyone else. Until we are able to list our talents, our gifts, and our strengths, we will not be able to cross over to serving others and moving toward significance and legacy. What if we all showed up knowing how we can contribute and make a difference?

Service is the key to sharing your abilities, strengths, and gifts. Speaking greatness and building others up creates value and gives others the opportunity to see their value. So many do not know their worth. They don't understand they have been given unique gifts to share with all those whose paths they cross, and by taking the time to name them, share them, and speak life into individuals, they are given hope and encouragement that they can be, do, and have all they have been created to do! Investments in the lives of others are like flat rocks you launch intentionally across a smooth lake. The rocks (investments in the lives of others) create circles of influence. The circles of influence impact others through time.

Live your HeartWork!

Do you know what your
calling—your HeartWork—is?
Take the journey. Do the work!
The investment in YOU is worth it!
Your passion will lead you to your purpose.
Your purpose will open doors to the connections
you need to live the work of your heart!
Be available, be willing,
and be obedient to the call!
Listen to the whispers of your heart!
Life's greatest beauty is found
in being in the service of others.
Live today. Let your HeartWork shine!
The individuals we serve become
our investment, Our calling,
Our life's HeartWork!

♥ Maximize Your Impact!

GAIL CARLOCK, OWNER and CEO of HeartWork Inspires, with her 28 years of medical device leadership and sales experience, lives her passion and purpose. Gail is a Ziglar Certified Trainer, who has worked with companies like DuPont, Guidant, Medtronic, St. Jude, Abbott, Marine Max, and Poly Lift to help their teams have transparent conversations that drive results and impact lives.

Gail is a future-focused, hope-based, energy engager, who happens to be a master relationship builder that speaks greatness into others. HeartWork Inspires focuses on capturing the hearts of individuals and teams while holding them accountable!

HeartWork is impactful!

Encountering everyday moments with a contagious enthusiasm for life, seeking kindness in others, and appreciating all we have releases power! HeartWork will give passionate, transformative power that changes how we show up in our lives and how we experience our days. HeartWork is a discipline, a choice to recognize, to record, and to remember our life moments.

Taking the time to reflect on what we are thankful for shows us that HeartWork is not a feeling. It is an act of choosing to be your best in all circumstances.

May your HeartWork equip, empower, and inspire others to have an impactful life!

To Contact Gail:

Cell 573-356-3532

Heartworkinspires@gmail.com

Opt In for a free download of the

The Impact Leadership Model

www.gailcarlock.com

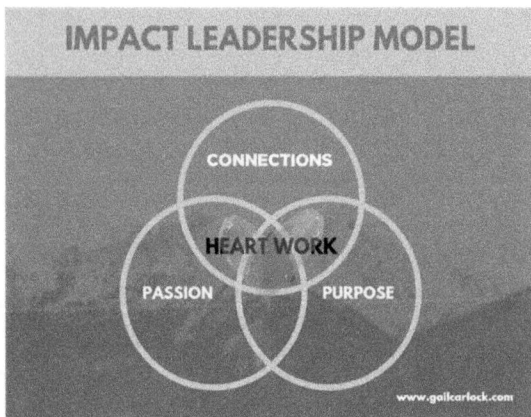